In And Out The Dugout

In And Out The Dugout

The Encyclopedia of Street Life

Cathy Howard

C/H Publishing

Copyright © 2004 by Cathy Howard

All rights reserved. This book is protected under the copyright law of the United States of America. No portion of this book may be reproduced or transmitted in any form except for the brief quotations in printed review, without the prior written permission of the author/publisher.

Published by Cathy Howard

Printed and bound in the United States of America by Record Printing

The original names have been changed to protect their identity

All scriptures from "New Living Translations"

For more information or questions concerning this book:
Cathy Howard
P.O. Box 23216
Belleville, Ill. 62226
Email-CTHOWAR7 @ aol.com
TheDugout7@netzero.com

Special Dedication

With sincere love and appreciation, I dedicate this book to my spiritual mother, Co- Pastor Patricia Phillips. Mother, words cannot express the appreciation and love in my heart for you. I often tell you that if you had been in my life years ago, my life would not have taken the turn it did, I learned that God restores and replaces what's missing in people's lives. What was missing in my life He replaced with you. You have brought the best out of me. You showed me how to stand and to walk as a virtuous woman. You share your life story to deliver and to free women who live in captivity. Your walk with Christ has inspired me and brought correction in my life. You took the time to talk to me and to show me the differences between Body Beauty and Lady Virtuous. I will always live as a virtuous woman. Thank you for being the precious jewel in my life. I will always love and respect you.

In and Out The Dugout

Table of Contents

Introduction	3
Chapter 1.........When It All Started	7
Chapter 2.........The Games Begin	14
Chapter 3.........You Would Think: Older and Better	22
Chapter 4.........The Table Has Turned	25
Chapter 5.........Where is Cathy?	32
Your Time of Decision	49
Life Exposures	52
#1 Young Lady	52
#2 Single Man	54
#3 Married Man	55
#4 I Took Him from His Wife	56
#5 Player	57
#6 Old Man Who Looks for a Young Prey`	59
#7 My First Boyfriend	60
#8 He Got A Child While We Were Dating	62

#9 We Live Together	63
#10 He Raped Me	65
#11 My Man Is In Prison (He has 20 years to life)	67
#12 He Beat Me But He Loves Me	68
#13 Your Girlfriend Who You Talk To	69
#14 Your Friend's Boyfriend	70
#15 The Young Man's Mother	72
#16 That's My Baby's Daddy	73
Ready To Give Up Your Past	75
The Change	77
Respect	78
Repentance	80
Jesus	83

Introduction

I'm a young black lady who was inspired by God to write about the obstacles that happened in my life. The title "In and Out the Dugout" came from God. God gave me the name in a series of dreams. This may sound strange to you, but God does speak to both women and men in dreams. There's even a scripture in the Bible where God says that *In the last days, I will pour out my Spirit upon all people. Your sons and daughters will prophesy, your young men will see visions and your old men will dream dreams. (Acts 2:17)* You see, you don't have to be a man for God to speak to you in a dream.

In my dreams, I saw different baseball teams. It showed me in the dugout on the wrong team, and I was never called to play in the game. There was man in all black who kept me out of sight. I felt that he was holding me hostage in the dugout only being used. It was later that I realized that the man in black was Satan. The bottom line is that Satan keeps us in a position where no one can see the greatness that God put in us. Satan's design for our lives is to keep us in captivity and to destroy our lives.

It was in another dream where I saw myself on another team. On this team, I was called to play. Our team was losing even though the bases were loaded. When I went up to bat, I hit a grand slam which brought everybody in, and we won the game. This dream showed me on God's winning team. Not only did I get an opportunity to play, but I was able to bring in the other people. That's out of the dugout.

When I repented and accepted Jesus Christ into my life, He changed me and gave me a new life in Him. **Who is this that those who become Christians become a new person? They are not the same anymore for the old life is gone. A new life has begun. All this newness of life is from God, who brought us back to himself through what Christ did. And God has given us the task of reconciling people to Him. (2Corinthians 5:17-18) Once you give your life to Christ, you are able to bring in the other people with the same DNA that you once had.**

Studying the meaning of two key words: *In* and *Dugout* gave me a clearer understanding of why Satan wanted to keep me in captivity. *In* means those who repeat or enter a repeated cycle , and *Dugout* means a holding place where one waits when not in a game. It also describes one being in a pit of hell. Satan knew if I were introduced to a new life, it will help destroy his kingdom.

When I came out of the pit, I didn't come out empty-handed. I came out with the master key to unlock the door and to expose the demons that seek to destroy all generations. I was like the person in the scripture who said, " I **waited patiently for the Lord to help me, and He turned to me and heard my cry. He lifted me out of the pit of despair, out of the mud and the mire. He set my feet on solid ground and steadied me as I walked along." (Psalm 40:1-2).**

As you journey through my life, journey through your life and prepare to expose and to defeat Satan. If you're ready to come out of the dugout, let the journey begin.

In and Out The Dugout

Chapter 1
When It All Started

My family was living on Carter Street in Washington Park, Illinois, when things started happening to me. I had eight brothers and sisters and we were all raised by both of our parents, but my relationship with my mom wasn't the best in the world. My dad was struggling from paycheck to paycheck just to make ends meet, and I can even remember cleaning houses after school to have lunch money. Even though things were really rough growing up, I can still remember the good times when I was running up and down the street playing with different kids in the neighborhood.

Then one day, I met this girl named Sally. Sally's mom, Mary, was a single parent, but she still was able to give Sally the very best. They had a beautiful house in a nice neighborhood, and there was always more than enough food to eat. Sally and her mom even had a big television set. I had not seen anything like it before because our television was the size of a matchbox, and everybody in our family would be huddling up together trying to see that little bitty screen. But that wasn't even all! Sally had more clothes than she could possibly wear, and it seemed like she had everything a girl could ever want. Coming from a poor family, this was my first time seeing the difference between having and not having.

After a while, Sally and I became very good friends, and her mother let me stay at their house night after night. We started going different places together like skating and going to the movies, which was the number one thing to do on the weekend. Before long, Mary treated me like I was a part of their family. She became more than a friend; she was the mother I needed. As far as Mary was concerned, I was her daughter. She took on the expense for my activities, and even made arrangements so Sally and I could go to school together.

As the school year progressed, Sally met a guy named Marcus. Marcus was a live wire, and would do anything at anytime. But at the same time, he was a handsome player. So much so, that by the end of the school year, Sally was calling Marcus her boyfriend.

During the summer months, we liked to go out and party. We really had the freedom to do whatever we wanted to do because Sally's mom had an active life and went on a lot of trips. Most of the time, we had the house to ourselves. So, partying was taken to another level and Marcus introduced Sally to alcohol, narcotics, and sex.

When the summer ended, Sally's high school life has begun. Sally went to Lincoln Senior High School, and the following year I went to East St. Louis High Senior High

School on the other side of town. Though Sally and I went to different schools, her mother showed no difference in how she looked out for us. Mary would take me to school even though it was of her way. Mary would even give me money to catch the city bus on days she had to be at work early. If it hadn't been for Mary, I wouldn't have an education.

Unfortunately, by the end of Sally's senior year of high school, she got pregnant by Marcus. Mary took this news hard, but she still saw to it that I got my education. During prom time, she even made sure that I had the proper attire.

Before the school year ended, I applied to many colleges, but only one accepted me, and that was Lincoln University in Jefferson City, Missouri. When the school year ended for me, Jackie, my oldest sister, and my father were the only family members present at my graduation. My real mother was busy running the streets as usual.

After high school, life took another turn. Mary met a man named Randy. Randy and Mary became so close he moved in with her. The summer had ended and it was time for me to go to college, but my family was unable to pay for my tuition. So my dad sat me down and explained how he wasn't able to send any of his kids off to college, but he would sacrifice to send me to beauty school.

While attending beauty school, Mary wasn't able to take me back and forth to school. So, I bought a car from a guy for three hundred dollars. I didn't even know how to drive yet, but I learned fast.

One day Mary went out of town leaving Sally and me at home. When I came home from school one evening, Sally was having an outdoor cookout and Marcus and his friends were there. Marcus was drinking heavily and acting like a party animal. Soon we were playing a game called "Faces." The object of the game was to see if you could keep up or correctly repeat the moves of the person before you. If you couldn't, then you would have to drink a shot of liquor. After playing the game and losing so many times, I had become heavily intoxicated. So, I went downstairs into the basement and fell asleep. By this time, Marcus had gotten Sally so high from drugs and alcohol she didn't know where she was in this world.

When I got up the next morning, all of my clothes were on the floor and blood was all over the sheet. My mind was in a daze, and the only things I could remember was hearing the microwave bell going off and the voice of Marcus's best friend, saying that he would kill me if I opened my mouth to anyone. All I knew for sure was that when I went to sleep, I was a virgin, but when I woke up, someone had taken advantage of me. So, I thought that it must have been Mark.

When I got my clothes on and went upstairs, Sally was in the kitchen. I asked her," Where is Mark?" and she said,

"Mark is gone. Why are you asking?" Before I could even answer, Marcus came out of the bedroom with a funny look on his face. I didn't know what to do so I went to my parents' house feeling very badly, not knowing what was wrong with me. I still hadn't gotten a chance to see Mark to ask him why he said that he would kill me. Or was I dreaming?

    A few days later, Marcus saw me and asked me to stop by his mother's house because he needed to talk to me about something. The next day I went to see Marcus, not knowing what he was going to tell me. I'll never forget the words that he said to me that day, "Remember the night of the party? It was not Mark who took advantage of you. It was me." At that time, my heart could have stopped beating. Marcus went on to tell me that he was not sorry for what he had done. In fact, he said that he really enjoyed every moment.

    For days after that, I was sick. I was trying to finish beauty school, but my mind wasn't there. I started staying away from Sally's house because after hearing what Marcus had said, I didn't know how to tell Sally the truth about what had happened to me because I knew that she was so in love with Marcus.

    Keeping this horrible secret to myself was mentally hurting me. I needed someone to talk to, so I turned to my sister, Nancy. I told her what had happened to me and she was outdone. I told her to promise me she wouldn't say anything about it, but days later Nancy and I had gotten into a fight. Her way of getting me back was to tell Sally my secret.

After getting out of school a few days later, I went over Sally's house not knowing my sister had told her about what had happened. I couldn't even get into the door good before Sally asked, "Did Marcus rape you?" All of a sudden I realized that my sister had told Sally what she promised me she would never tell. To make it worse, Marcus was right there as Sally asked me about the incident. At that time I didn't have a chance. So, I told her to ask Marcus. But instead of doing that, she began to call me all kinds of nasty names and told me to get out of her house and to never come back. As I walked out of the house, tears rolled down my face, and I didn't open my mouth to say one word. By the time I got home, Nancy had moved to New York with her boyfriend, Brad. I was too scared to talk to anyone else, so I isolated myself from everybody.

Not long after that day, I ran into Sally and Marcus again when I was driving my sister, Jane, to my grandmother's house. I got out of the car and Sally asked, "Lynn, did Marcus rape you?" Just like before, I told Marcus to tell Sally what he did to me. He sat there looking crazy and didn't say a word. Sally said she should get out of the car and kick my butt. Then, Marcus stopped Sally from fighting me by saying that it was not worth it. As they drove away, I finally understood how Sally was so brainwashed by Marcus. Yet, I still couldn't believe she picked him over a true friendship.

Chapter 2
The Games Begin

Years later, things had really changed in my life. My life no longer revolved around Sally and her mom. I had lost all contact with them and the only people from my past that were a part of my new life were Mark and Mary's boyfriend, Randy. I could always count on Randy to be there for me and to help me out whenever I needed him. Other than that, I started meeting new people and looking for love in all the wrong places. Even after experiencing the tragedy of rape, partying was still the number one thing in my life.

At a house party that a guy named Brandon was having, I met his older brother, Jerome, who had moved here from Texas. When I walked into the party, people were dancing, drinking and playing pool. After being in the party for a while, I decided to play pool. When it was my turn to play, Jerome wanted to hold a conversation. When the party was over, Jerome wanted to finish our conversation at a later time, so we exchanged numbers.

As time went on, Jerome and I decided to spend more time together. Soon we started hanging out and going to the movies. Jerome was a giving person and would go out of his way to make me happy. Yet, my past was still controlling my life, and I wasn't about to trust anyone because I didn't know how to let go of the hurt. So, the pain of abandonment and betrayal started to affect the relationship I had with Jerome.

Meanwhile, Randy and I became more than friends. Randy spoiled me with his attention, his money, and his conversation. I was just drawn to him like a magnet because he'd always been there for me. We would meet each other in secret places, but there would also be times when he came over to my house. We were doing a good job of keeping our relationship private until one day when Mark called me and Randy picked up the phone. It concerned me that now someone else knew about our relationship. However, I felt that as long as Jerome never found out, everything would work out fine.

One day I ran into Debbie, an old friend from high school. We talked about old times, went to parties, and all sorts of different places. When I introduced her to Jerome, I was glad that they got along. I thought that I had finally found another true friend. The only problem was that Jerome and Debbie became so close that they slept together. After I confronted them about their secret relationship, Debbie came clean and told Jerome to tell the truth. Jerome just stood there with this dumbfounded look on his face. At that moment I had a flashback of the episode that took place between Marcus, Sally and me.

After my moment of frustration was over, I decided to remain neutral because I didn't want to let history repeat itself. So, even though he cheated on me, I decided to still stay in a relationship with Jerome, but the catch was that now I wasn't going to ever trust anyone again or feel guilty about doing my own thing.

Months later, I found out I was pregnant. I was so undecided on having a baby that I was going to have an abortion. As I was leaving out the back door of my parent's house to meet my friend LaDonna at the abortion clinic, my dad knocked on my bedroom window saying he needed to talk to me. He said that the Lord told him that I was pregnant and was planning on having an abortion, and that if I have one, I wasn't going to live. Then, my dad told me a story about a tree that couldn't bear fruit. He said, "The fruit tree was put on Earth to bring forth fruit. Some trees bare fruit before time. Some don't ever bring forth fruit. The tree is there, but for some odd reason it's not able to bear fruit. If you have this baby, your tree will produce fruit for generations to come." He ended our conversation by saying that if I had the baby, he would do all that he could to help me.

I didn't know much about God back then, but something inside told me to trust in what my dad was saying. So, I changed my mind about the abortion and told Jerome I was carrying his child. At first, he was very angry, but after a few weeks, Jerome accepted the fact that I was pregnant and was ready to take on full responsibility of being a father. The only bad part about it all was that when Jerome told his mother that I was pregnant, she said that if it was true, it was going to be a hard pill to swallow.

As the weeks went on, Jerome began to ask me about a man named Darrel. I told him I didn't know what he was talking about. Little did I know that the Darrel that Jerome was asking me about was really Randy. But even his suspicions didn't stop Jerome from taking good care of me. He visited my job on a regular basis and made sure that I had food to eat every day because it was very hard for me to leave the salon. I had so many customers and was working so hard and that was not a good thing to do while being pregnant.

One day I went to use the ladies' room and saw blood in the toilet. I told the lady who I worked for that I had came on my cycle. She told me that I was pregnant and I didn't have a cycle. I called the doctor's office, and they told me to come to the office right away.

Before I went to the doctor office, I stopped at the corner store to get a juice. As I was coming out of the store, Randy was getting out of his car. He stopped me and touched my stomach. The baby kicked so hard that I went down to my knees. It scared me so bad that I got in my car as fast as I could as Randy called out after me,
"What's wrong with you?" I said nothing and drove away.

In and Out The Dugout

When I got to the doctor's office, the doctor told me that I would have to stay in the hospital over the weekend for further examination. I immediately called my father and Jerome to tell them I was in the hospital. What I didn't know was that at the same time, Mark ran into Debbie and told her that I was secretly seeing Randy. She liked Jerome so much that she went and told him what happened.

After a week went by, I started dreaming about being in labor and having a little white girl. Then, the second week I was in the hospital, I had the baby. After giving birth I didn't get a chance to see the baby because I was in so much pain.

When my mother came to see the baby and me, she rushed in to my room and said, "Lynn, this baby doesn't have a black spot on him." So, when my mother left the hospital, I asked the nurse to direct me to the nursery. That's when I saw my baby for the first time. It wasn't a little white girl; it was a little white boy.

At first, I was shocked because before that very moment, I had always thought that Jerome was the father. There was so much going through my mind. I didn't know how I was going to face Jerome after he'd been there for me throughout the entire pregnancy, and I didn't want to hurt him even though he had hurt me. At the same time, I knew that people would think what they wanted to think about my having a baby by a white man, but that still didn't make me ashamed that my baby was biracial. So, a few hours later I called someone very close to me and told him to tell Randy that he was the father on my son.

    When LaDonna came over to see me in the hospital, she awakened me after visiting the baby in the nursery and said to me as if I did not know, "Girlfriend, that baby is white." So, I told her about the father of my child. By the time I got out of the hospital, she had told over half the city that Randy was my baby's daddy.

    By that time, I found out that Jerome also knew that I had the baby and he wasn't the father. Jerome's father and brother continued talking to me. They said that mistakes happen and that they knew that I wasn't trying to hurt Jerome. When I finally left the hospital, my son could not leave with me. He had to stay in the hospital for two weeks while I returned to work early to make a life for us.

    After picking my son up from the hospital, another level of hell started in my life. Someone hated me so bad that when I got out of my car and went into the salon, someone threw a firebomb in my car. My first thought was that it was Jerome, but I found out that he had married a girl out of town. I wondered if he was still holding on to memories of me in his heart. I didn't understand why our relationship had taken such a bad turn.

    One day I was riding down the street, and Mark pulled me over and asked me if he could see the baby. I finally got a chance to ask him why he told Debbie about my secret.

He said that he didn't know that it was going to affect so many people's lives. Then, he apologized and drove off shaking his head. For once, it was nice to have someone actually be sorry for causing me so much pain. After that, even Marcus tried to make up for the hurt he caused me by helping me financially. He was doing for my son what his own father refused to do.

During a dream one night, I was eating some Chinese food. The next day Marcus called me at work and said Mark had gotten killed at the rice house. I told Marcus he was telling a lie. I went to Marcus's job to see his expression on his face. Right then I knew he was telling the truth. That day left two people looking for comfort in all the wrong places.

Shortly thereafter, I had moved into my first apartment and was taking care of my son the best way I knew how. Marcus had gone on to marry Sally and started a family. A year later, Randy married Mary.

After all Mary had done for me, I didn't want to make her life worse by dragging her husband through court and embarrassing her in a legal battle. But I needed help. So, my next step was to try to get my son some help from his dad the legal way. I took him to court and in front of the judge he said my son wasn't his child. I couldn't believe he let those words come out of his mouth. So, the judge ordered a paternity test that day and scheduled another court date as soon as possible. When we returned to court, the paternity test confirmed with 99.5% degree of certainty that Randy was the father of my child. Therefore, the judge ordered Randy to pay child support.

After going to court with Randy, I really wanted to stop the cycle of pain in my life. Well, what I wanted for my life was totally different than what I was able to achieve. Despite all of my struggles, all I did was pause a moment, catch my breath, ... and then just enter the same cycle of pain and confusion at a different level.

Chapter 3
You Would Think: Older is Better

Another level of hell started in my life when I started going to different clubs. Going out clubbing and meeting new people began to take the place of the hurt I felt inside. I was living the life of a single lady and playing by my own rules.

Entering a new level of the same old cycle, I started dating, Sam, a married man. I convinced myself that dating a married man was convenient because I wasn't committing myself to anyone. Sam was an older guy who was experienced. His experience trapped me in a level that I never dreamed of entering.

Sam was the kind of man who knew how to make a lady feel important. Coming from under so much hurt, I needed to feel important just one time in life. That was the wrong mindset for me to have, especially since Sam was a gambler and an alcoholic. Going through so much hell in the past, gambling and social drinking became tools of relaxation for me.

Sam's way of life was very different from my own, and he began introducing me to several of his friends. After getting to know me, they encouraged me to move on with my life, but I was just too attached to Sam. Anyway, how could his friends even begin to know the things that I had gone through in my life? How could they think I could live without Sam when he had started playing such a very important role in my life? So, I didn't listen to his friends even though they had known Sam much longer than me. I just totally ignored them.

Well, it didn't take long before I found out for myself that someone else was in Sam's life and it wasn't his wife. It was another woman who had been in his life years before I entered. Sam kept this a secret, but the women found out about me. Like a bad dream, things started happening to me all over again. The woman was putting my car on a flat and writing letters pretending like she was Sam's wife. But all the while, Sam was the type of person that if he did something, he would make up. He knew how to keep a lady's mouth closed.

To my surprise, there came a day when even Sam couldn't take it anymore. When he came over to my house, he said that I was a beautiful person and I deserved more than a married man. He confessed about all that he had done, said he was sorry and ended our relationship.

When Sam walked out the door, I understood, too, how the relationship had gotten out of hand. I also recognized that I had a son and that my son needed a mother. Even though I was hurt so deeply, I knew that Sam had done the right thing by telling me the truth and by moving on with his life. Still my heart was crushed, and I felt like I had nowhere to turn and no one to cry to for help. Just then, when I was about to give up, my good friend, Regina, came all the way from Ohio to help me pick up the pieces of my life and to find hope.

Chapter 4
The Table Has Turned

    The next layer of hell started in my life when I ran into Jerome whose wife had left him. Knowing the pain and the vengeance he had in his heart, I still decided to start a new relationship with him. I later realized the mistake I made when he showed me how he was so full of revenge. He'd make people pay for past disappointments rather than forgive them. He just couldn't see the good qualities in a person.

    After being back in the relationship with Jerome for a few months, I started to see all the pain and hurt he had in his heart. He was talking about all of the things he did to his wife because of the pain I had caused him. He said that his biggest hurt was when he found out that my son wasn't his child. Jerome's wife just couldn't take the mental and verbal abuse. So, one day when he was at work, she emptied the house and moved back to Utah.

    Because I had caused him so much pain in the last affair, Jerome didn't trust me. I kept on hoping one day he would see a change that I had made in my life, but he just couldn't see past all of the hurt and heartache. This time he accused me of cheating when I was serious about the relationship. His insecurities became so strong that he started stalking me and he and his mother were accusing me of

In and Out The Dugout

things that were not taking place. After awhile, it was clear that Jerome was out for revenge and I didn't have a way out of this relationship. What scared me even more was the fact that Jerome was a prison guard and carried a gun to work.

One morning my fears became reality when Jerome got off work and came by the house. I was fast asleep and my son was lying by my side. When Jerome looked through the window and saw movement in the bed, he knocked on the door. Half asleep, I opened the door and Jerome was right there with a gun in my face saying, "If a man is in your bed, I'm going to kill the both of you." I begged him not to kill my son. Jerome yanked back the covers and saw my son asleep in the bed. He apologized, but right then and there, the trust was gone. Jerome had become a mad man out of control.

However, I continued the relationship, I was looking for an exit every day because I knew that this level of hell could cost me my life. One night, Jerome and I went to the club and he said that he felt like killing me because I had caused so much pain in his life. He said that he just couldn't function in any relationship because of the memories in his mind. Just after Jerome had finished telling me how he felt, a man walked up and gave me his number. I was so outdone that I sat there and didn't say a word. Jerome was upset beyond belief. He raised hell all night, accusing me of letting the man disrespect him. His way of getting back at me was forcing me to repeatedly have sex with him. It was like being raped over and over again.

Even though I knew that Jerome was out of control, I didn't have anyone to help me. My neighbor would often tell me that a man was checking my windows every night, and even one of Jerome's friends warned me about Jerome driving past my house. He said that Jerome told him that if he saw a car in the yard after nine o'clock, he would shoot the house up and kill everyone inside.

Finally, I realized that if I was going to survive and protect my son, I would have to take drastic action. So, a few days later, I decided to leave my home after only living there six months. For my safety, I would tell Jerome that I was moving back to my parents' house when actually....I was on the run.

On the day I moved, someone called Jerome at work and told him that a moving van was outside my home. When he got off work, he came straight to my house in his uniform. He asked, "Where are you moving to?" Just like I had planned, I told him," To my parents' home." I could see how angry he was, but by this time I was just so scared of him that I just didn't care what I had to do to get away from him.

Unfortunately, it didn't end there because Jerome followed the moving van to the storage bin. He harassed the movers as they were working asking them which one of them was dating me. The movers tried their best to just ignore

Jerome, and they warned me that I needed to get rid of him and fast.

At this point, I realized that Jerome was obsessed with hurting me no matter what. On the inside, I was a nervous wreck. I just wanted out! Though I was numb all over, I knew that on the outside, I couldn't show any signs of weakness. That was just street life.

Not long after that episode, Jerome met a girl named Janet. His plan was to hurt me with the girl. If only he knew how glad I was that he had moved on with someone else. For the next few weeks, I moved into a hotel with my son. Finally I felt relieved.

Though I worked every day, I couldn't afford to continue to stay at the hotel and save up for an apartment at the same time. All of a sudden, the peace that I had began to crumble. The price of leaving my home and everything else that I owned was more than I was prepared to face. Even though I had escaped from Jerome, I still had no freedom. Jerome had one controlling power in my life and that was money. The only way I knew how to make it was through his financial means. The pain of trying to survive began to dictate my judgment. I felt that I couldn't live without him. Feeling like I was at a dead end, I found myself right back at his door. I tried so hard to escape this relationship, but it wouldn't let me go.

Jerome accepted me back, but it wasn't without a cost.

In and Out The Dugout

One day while I staying in his home, the phone rang; it was his girlfriend. After he finished talking to her on the phone, he exploded because he wanted to be with her, but I was in the way. After we argued, I asked him to take me to my parents' house. The entire way there all he could talk about was the things in the past. All I could think about was that maybe down deep inside I didn't really want to let Jerome move on. I kept telling myself that I was glad that he had a girlfriend. But at the same time, I was having a hard time accepting it because I was so deeply confused, not just with the fact that he had a girlfriend but with myself. If I was so afraid of Jerome, why did I keep running back to him? Could it be *me* that didn't know how to let *him* go?

With all of these mixed emotions going on in my mind, I was worn out when I finally got to my parents' house. I told him that we would talk tomorrow. I got out of the truck to go in the house when Jerome told me if I went in, he would shoot me in the back of the head. When I turned around, I was staring down the barrel of his gun. Jerome told me to get back in the truck, and he took me back to his house, locked me in and raped me all night.

The nightmare didn't stop there. He started calling and coming to my job on a regular basis checking to see if I was at work... I felt trapped. I was also humiliated by the different women he would put in my face to make me jealous.

In and Out The Dugout

One day he decided to have a birthday party for the both of us. He told me that he would invite all the people to the party. I knew that wouldn't work. So, I told him to go have the party without me.

On the night of the party, I went to a nightclub. I wanted to get drunk and to try to forget all of the things I was going through in my life. I was sitting at the bar when Sam, my old friend, walked into the club. He sat down and we started talking. When Jerome walked in the club with Janet to make me jealous, it backfired in his face. After that night, I knew that Jerome was out for more than revenge, and he wouldn't care what he had to do to get it.

Working hard trying to take care of my son, I needed some rest and living from place to place wasn't working out for me. One day I decided to rent another hotel room; that same day Jerome called on my cell phone and wanted to know what I was doing. I told him that I was sleeping. What I didn't know was that someone had told him that they saw my car at the hotel. After a couple hours of rest, I got up and went to the ATM machine to get some money for some food. Jerome pulled up at the ATM machine with tears in his eyes. He began to tell me how I messed his life up. He knew that he was out of control and needed some help but his pride got in the way. Letting out all of his anger, Jerome beat me and beat me. He seemed to be getting a joy out of hurting me. Blow by blow, he reminded me how I messed his life up getting pregnant by another man, and a white man at that. He was screaming about how his wife left him because she knew his heart was somewhere else.

When he left the parking lot, I called the police. The officer asked me, "Did someone rape you?" After giving the report, the officer said, "If you press charges, he will be a victim on his job." I knew that if Jerome went to prison, he would be assaulted by the same prisoners that he guarded. At that very moment, a greater reward than pressing charges was having the power to finally break free from Jerome.

Before the officer left, he said that he would make sure that Jerome would stay away from me, and that he was going over to talk with him that night.

The next day I got a call from a client who wanted to make an appointment. I told her that I wouldn't be able to work for a while because of what had happened. She asked me the guy's name, and when I told her, she knew his mother from work.

The next thing I know, Jerome's mother called me asking, "How much money would it take for you to stay out of my son's life?" She said that she would be willing to pay the price because she didn't want her son to lose his job. I told her to take the money and get her son some help. I let her know that I would be okay as long as she could keep him away from me. She said, "Thank you" and hung up the phone.

Chapter 5
Where Is Cathy?

A month after the break up with Jerome, I moved into my own apartment. I had to try and make it on my own because living at home with my parents was difficult. My mother didn't understand the things I was going through simply because she was too busy sending my dad through situations. My dad didn't have any say-so in the house. I was seeking peace and I couldn't find it there.

With a new start on life, I decided not to date. I wanted to raise my son in a healthy environment so that he would not think a man was supposed to treat a woman badly. I changed the things in my life that would make me a good mother. My son and I were doing things together, and I enjoyed the time I was spending with him.

After a long day, I stopped in the barbershop on the corner of 39th Street to get my son's hair cut. The barber did such an excellent job that I decided that I would surely go back to that barber not only for my son but for myself. So, a few weeks later, I took time off work on my birthday to pay bills and to get a haircut. After getting my haircut, the barber, Clifford, followed me out to my car and gave me his telephone number. After going through so much hell with Jerome you would think I had gone through enough, but for some reason, I made the decision to take a chance again. After several dates with Clifford, we developed a special friendship. In fact, my son liked Clifford so much that he told him he wished he had a dad like him.

In the first year of our relationship, Clifford was such a perfect gentleman. Though Clifford had several kids from different relationships, I couldn't find anything wrong with him. We spent lots of time together, and Clifford showed me things I'd never seen. Clifford was the kind of man who loved to go places. Even my father approved of him. Clifford was also close with his family, so I met them as well. I was especially close to his mother.

After a year had passed, the relationship with Clifford became serious, and I had developed feelings for him. At the same time, new things about Clifford had come out. Clifford, the perfect gentleman, turned out to be married. He even had another girlfriend named Jennifer. Now after all of the previous wrong relationships I'd had, you would think that I would have become strong enough to walk away, but another crisis in my life kept me from dealing with Clifford, his wife, and his woman.

The crisis began several years earlier when my brother was sentenced to 12 months and 1 day in prison which amounted to 10 months in federal prison. My mother had never had one of her children to go to jail, so she made a deal with God. She told God that she would come off the streets if He kept Roni out of jail. Well, she came off the streets, but my brother still went to jail.

When my brother got out of jail, he still continued the same lifestyle. Once when my mother was going to visit my sister in New York for Thanksgiving, Roni took her to the bus station. That was the last time I remember seeing my brother alive. Then, a few days before Thanksgiving, my son woke up out of his sleep and told me to cook dinner for Thanksgiving. He said that Papa and Uncle Roni needed something to eat for the holiday. Listening to my son really paid off because I actually did cook dinner for them, not knowing the night after Thanksgiving, my brother would be killed.

On the very night my brother died, I had a vision. First, the phone rang. When I answered it, no one said a word. The second time it rang, again...no one said anything. All of a sudden, I saw smoke begin to fill the room as if someone was smoking. Then, I smelled Roni's scent so strong that it felt like he was right there in the room with me. Just then, the phone rang for the third time, and it was my niece. She told me that I needed to come over my dad's house quick. I hung up the phone and rushed to my dad's house thinking something was wrong with my son who was spending the night there.

When I arrived at my dad's house, there was something black hovering over the house. Then, Dad opened the door and said, "Roni was killed on the highway." Without even taking the time to think or to respond to what my dad had just said, I jumped back in my car and drove to the highway. When I got there, I saw my Dad's van and it was totaled. At first, the police wouldn't let me through until one of the policemen I knew said, "Let her through. That's his sister." The police let me know Roni was taken to the hospital.

Walking into the hospital, I noticed that the floor was so cold. That's when I realized that I had been in such a daze that I hadn't even put on any shoes. Suddenly, a policeman came to me and said, "Your brother's gone home." I said, "What? Now wait until I get home and tell my dad that somebody's had the nerve to call him saying Roni's dead." As I turned to walk out the door, the policeman grabbed me and hugged me tight and said, "No, sweetheart, I mean your brother went to his heavenly home."

Before I could even catch my breath, another policeman told me that I needed to identify the body. As soon as they led me to the morgue and removed the sheet from over my brother's face, I passed out. When I finally came to, my older brothers had gotten to the hospital and we signed the papers for the autopsy.

After we left the hospital, we went back to my dad's house. My dad wanted us to call my mom and see if she wanted to be flown back from New York. When my mother heard my voice, she said, "What happened to Roni?" I told her that he'd been killed. She refused my dad's offer to fly her home and said that she'd catch the bus home because she needed to have a talk with Jesus.

Soon the morning came and Clifford called. When I told him what had happened, he came over right away and that was when the door opened wide again for Clifford to become a comforter in my life. At that very moment, I decided to ignore the fact that he had a wife and a girlfriend.

Because of the death of my brother, I had fallen apart again. Roni and my father had been the only family members I could count on, and with Roni gone, Clifford became more than a lover. He was my hope. Not only that, but he became so close to my family that they saw him as the brother we were missing. Even though my relationship with Clifford was all wrong, I didn't know how to stop depending on him for strength.

Trying to come to terms with Roni's death, I had a talk with my dad about the last days of my brother's life. I wanted to know if Roni had eaten the Thanksgiving meal I cooked for him and dad. Dad said that Roni kept eating it all day long like he knew it was going to be his last meal. A preacher had even told my dad that Roni said that he was going to die in all black and that's exactly what he had on...down to his underwear.

A few days after Roni's burial, I had a dream. Two men in black were in the front seat of a car and Roni and I were in the backseat. As we drove along, my brother started crying. Then, he turned to me and said, "Go repent and get it right with God." Then, he pushed me out into green pastures.

After that dream, I started having a series of dreams and visions. I also began hearing all kinds of strange noises. I was so scared and confused because I didn't know what it all meant. Not knowing where to go or who to turn to, I leaned on Clifford. He was my crutch.

Months after my brother's death, my sister in New York was planning a big birthday party. Clifford and a few of his friends went to the party with me. Before we left, I had a dream that I passed out in a restaurant and was rushed to the hospital. I told Clifford's mom about the dream, but she told me to just pray and that our trip would be fine. When we arrived in New York, Clifford and I needed to get some sleep before the party. Before long, it was time for the party and things were going crazy.

When Clifford and I arrived at the party, I realized that Marcus was there also. He had chosen to travel to New York for his vacation and had heard about my sister's party and made his way there. When Clifford saw Marcus, he thought I had planned to meet him there. He even accused me of having a secret relationship with Marcus because one night when Sally saw us at a club back home, she told him to beware of me because I had slept with Marcus. She refused to tell Clifford the truth about what Marcus had done to me. So, Clifford saw Marcus as a threat to our relationship which made the whole night a disaster.

After a long weekend of partying, it was time to go home. Before getting on the highway, Clifford and I decided to stop at a restaurant to get something to eat. At the restaurant, Clifford passed out, and the dream I had about me came to pass, but in reverse. Instead of me, it was Clifford who was rushed to the hospital and released the same day.

After arriving back home, more hell broke loose. My dad was diagnosed with leukemia. Things were turning for the worst very fast; hell was breaking out on every corner. Trying to handle life's disappointments and my dad's illness, I couldn't find a way of escape.

Adding fuel to the fire, my son told me about a little girl at school who was always picking on him. I told him that the little girl was probably picking on him because he is handsome. He said, "No, mama this is different." Days later my son showed me the little girl. Her grandmother was picking her up from school. At that time, I didn't know the lady so I left it alone. As time went on, I saw the little girl with Jennifer, Clifford's other girlfriend. To keep peace, I told my son to stay away from the little girl.

With my son now involved in this mess, I thought I'd finally have enough strength to let Clifford go. So, I contacted Clifford and told him to stop by the house. After talking to him about the problem, he totally ignored the fact that my son was experiencing adult foolishness. Therefore, the problem was never squared away because Clifford never addressed the issue, and the little girl continued to pick on my son. Because my son was a little boy, I did not want him fighting or disrespecting little girls. I just told him to stay calm and to refuse to fight her because I knew that he would be a husband to a lady one day.

As time went on, I didn't even have peace on my job. One day a lady called my job and asked for Clifford. I was so outdone. I asked her to repeat the name of the person she was asking for and she said, "Clifford Patrick." When I asked who was calling, she said, "Jennifer." I told her, " I hope you find him before I do because if I find him before you, I'm kicking his BUTT." I had so much rage in me because I was tired of being disrespected.

Soon after I hung up the phone with Jennifer, Clifford called the salon by mistake because he had forgotten the number he had called. Clifford was getting all mixed up with his relationships. He was getting all three of us confused. By this time I was totally fed up, and I didn't have very much to say to him over the phone. However, I couldn't wait to get my hands on him. Since Clifford went to the gym every day and had left his gym bag in my car, I knew I'd see him before Jennifer would.

Sure enough, minutes after he called me, he had to contact me again because of the gym bag. When he called me, I met him halfway. I told him what happened, and he acted like he didn't know what I was talking about. I had to leave a mark on him so I slammed his leg in the car door.

Later that day, I realized that things were getting worse with Clifford by the minute, and I told him the things I was accepting from him were not normal. It felt like an OMEN had entered into my life. Yet in still, I stayed in the relationship for two more years.

In this phase of our relationship, going out of town became an event for us. One time my sister was having another party and this time Clifford wasn't able to go. Pretending to go wash my rental car for me before I left town, Clifford was gone for two days. When it was time for me to leave for New York, I called Clifford for the car. He hung the phone up on me.

Instead of asking me not to go to New York, Clifford took matters into his own hands. After arguing on the phone, I went to his job because I was more than ready to leave for New York. When I tried to get the car back, Clifford said he'd give me the car back later. Then, he got in the car, took off driving fast down the street, and the police stopped him because he had a warrant out for his arrest. I didn't make the trip to New York because he made a weekend trip turn into the weekend from hell.

In the fourth year of my relationship with Clifford, things had shifted to a level of hell for which there was no explanation. Going through so many levels of hell, I remembered what my dad had always told me, "Daughter you reap what you sow." I knew a change had to take place in my life. First, I moved out of my apartment because I developed a guilty conscience. I just felt that I was living too close to Clifford and I wanted to separate myself from him and be free from the madness.

Months after living in my new house, things really started turning for the worse. It seemed like my life was taken over by a demon. Right in front of my eyes, Clifford was changing into Sam, the gambler, from my past relationship. The only difference was that Clifford was acting as if he had no conscience at all. With Sam, I gambled to relax me, but with Clifford, it became a lifestyle. I learned the art of intense gambling. I was like a crack-head that needed some drugs. I wasn't able to sleep at night, and I thought I was hearing people knocking at my door.

One day, Clifford's mother called me at work and asked me to stop by her house on my way home. The reason why she wanted me to come was not to hurt me but to help me move on with my life. She said that Clifford had divorced his first wife and married Jennifer within two weeks of his divorce. She also told me that Jennifer was pregnant.

In and Out The Dugout

During the time when Clifford had gotten married, my dad had become very ill. Running back and forth to the hospital, I didn't have any time to confront Clifford about his new marriage, but I did tell my dad. After hearing that Clifford had gotten married and was about to become a dad for the fifth time, he said, "Do not walk away from Clifford." I knew that my father was a very wise man, yet I still I didn't understand the reason why my dad wanted me to stay with Clifford after what he did to me. I felt betrayed and very confused because I didn't understand the reason why my father said that. So, I stayed confused without an answer.

Ultimately, my life started going in a cycle. Old ways of life were recycling and thing were happening that I thought had past. I wanted to get revenge. Sometimes I would think of ways I could get back at Clifford for all of the hurts he'd caused me. I wanted someone to feel the pain that was inside of me. Clifford was adding more fuel to the fire that was burning in my soul. I was like a flaming demon that needed more gasoline to destroy everything in its path.

During that year my sister was having another party. The girls at the salon decided to take the trip to New York. The night I was leaving for New York, a friend stopped by the house to give me some money and to wish me a safe trip. A couple of minutes after he left the house, the doorbell rang. It was Clifford; he was sitting outside my house in a rental car watching the house.

He confronted me about the man and I confronted him about how he had gotten divorced and remarried all in less than two weeks. Finally, he told me he was going to get revenge because the man was over my house. I saw so many different sides of Clifford on that night that he reminded me of a psychopath.

Before leaving for New York that same night, I talked with Clifford, I told him he was the last married man I would date and that my lifestyle was going to change. When I got to New York, I told my sister that this was the last party I'd be coming to and that the next time I visited her, it would be to have a peaceful vacation.

After returning from New York, things continued happening to me that were very strange, and I was still hearing knocks on the door. Other changes in my life were for the better. I started walking in the park to lose weight. Likewise, I became very uncomfortable with the way people around me were talking. I was no longer interested in using or listening to bad language, hearing about going to nightclubs, and talking about sex. I was even praying and crying out to God to change my life. I realized that I hadn't had a good night's sleep in years. My life was like a merry-go-round.

Days later as I was walking in the park, I saw a man, woman, and a child and they reached out to hug me. The words they said to me were "you are on your way." I didn't understand what they were talking about so I continued walking. Something made me turn around, and when I did, I didn't see the people who had given me the hug. The feeling I had was very strange. So, I didn't finish my walk and went home. After arriving at work, I told the girls who worked with me that I was going to church. The girls gave me a very funny look and started laughing.

Two days later, a lady came in the salon and said she needed to talk to me. She told me she had a word from God for me. She said God told her to tell me to give it up and turn it over to Him. To make me know it was God she said that I had a lot of customers, but God made room so she could talk to me. She also told me about things in my life that you take to your grave with you. After I heard that, my hands went up in the air. I was ready to give it to God. She said, "Don't be ashamed of the tattoo on your chest," but she had no way of knowing about the tattoo if God hadn't told her because it wasn't even showing. When she left, the salon customers were coming from north, south, east and west.

At the end of the day, a client of another stylist came to the back and said the same thing to me. I told her about the lady earlier, and she was thanking the Lord. *I* told the Lord that I got the message. After that, Mrs. Dorothy Walker, a client, came in the salon talking to the ladies in the salon about God. I asked her to call me. After talking to me and praying for me, she invited me to her church.

Sunday morning I went to her church and the pastor was preaching the same thing the lady said at the salon. I got up when it was time to receive salvation and that day I gave my life to Christ. Suddenly I felt like the things I was going through were over. The weight of hopelessness was finally lifted from my shoulders and the shackles were taken off my feet.

By the grace of God, I slept for what seemed like five years in one night on the night of my salvation. It felt like I was sleeping in the middle of God's arms. It was a sleep and rest that I can't explain. The problems that were so hard for me to solve were so simple for God. The anger I had in my heart turned into peace.

On the second night of my salvation, I dreamed about my mother. When I woke up, I went over to her house, apologized and asked her to forgive me because I had favored my dad more than her. After that, I told the Lord I would apologize to everyone I had hurt because I didn't want my old life anymore.

When I accepted Christ, Clifford was the first one to go. The omen that I felt had controlled my life had no more authority over my life. Finally, I knew my life had truly changed when I saw Clifford and Jennifer at the movies and it didn't bother me. What was hard for me before was easy for God.

In and Out The Dugout

Just after being saved for one week, I was raped again in my home by a man that I knew. For once in my life, I felt hope only to have it shattered by another crisis. I couldn't believe what had happened to me. I was praying and telling the Lord that I didn't understand. I pleaded with the Lord, "Please do not take your peace from me." Then, I asked, "God, did you deliver me just to start this all over again?"

Like an answer to my prayer, Mrs. Dorothy Walker called the house right at that moment. She wanted to know if I wanted to go to church with her. I told her what happened and she said God was not going to leave me and that I was okay. She said that God saw what happened and was not going to take my joy. In fact, she said He is adding more.

When I got to church, Co-Pastor preached on repentance and the love of God and the very next day, the guy that had raped me left his wife and was on the airplane to Utah. God had removed that thorn out of my side. A day later Clifford came around testing God saying that the devil had power like God. Clifford was instantly moved out of my life.

On September 11, 2000, I was on the highway going to the doctor. At the doctor's office I had gotten ill and I had a mild stroke. Two hours later after leaving the doctor's office, I was admitted into the hospital. While I was in the hospital the Lord was working things out for my good. The Lord spoke to me and said, "This dad I gave to you was for a season, and he can't save you or heal you, only I can." Though my dad was the one I depended on a lot, I realized the difference between my natural father and my heavenly Father who supplies all of my needs according to His riches and glory. The Lord was setting me up in the hospital for a miracle.

When the doctor was taking me to the heart room to run tests, I felt a pair of hands on my head, and I started crying. The doctor told me not to move, but I wanted to let him know the feeling down my right side came back.

After the test, the nurse took me back to my room. My dad was waiting in the room when the doctor came in and sat on the bed. The doctor said, "The test came back negative. I don't know what happened to you." The next day I was released from the hospital. It was a miracle!

A month after I got out of the hospital, my dad had gotten ill. The Lord had showed me my dad in a dream. I saw the sky open up like a nucleus, and my dad went up into it. The nucleus was expanding and some people were going up into it with my dad while others were on Earth burning. By Christmas things had gotten rough for my dad, and on February 14th, Valentine's Day, my dad passed away. Glory had set in and God worked things out for the best.

Suddenly I realized that all of the dreams, visions, and other strange occurrences were God's way of reaching out to me and saving me from destruction. In the midst of all of the struggles and pain I had suffered, I didn't know who I was or where my life was headed. However, God knew who I was all the time and He had my destiny in His hands.

    Most precious of all was how God gave me a vision of my own brother coming back to warn me to give my life to Jesus before it was too late. I know now that the green pastures that Roni pushed me into were the green pastures God speaks of in the 23rd Psalm. Yes, the Lord *was* and still *is* my shepherd. He gives me peace and lets me lie down to rest in His green pastures. He restores my soul. I thank God for loving me enough to help me realize that the "old" me had to be killed so that the "new" me could live. I'm so glad that I was willing to die so that I can stay free and do the will of my Lord and Savior Jesus Christ.

Your Time of Decision

Now that you have read the synopsis of my life, the stage has been set for you to enter into the door of *Life Exposures*. Entering this door is hazardous because it will expose things and issues of life we take lightly. These issues may have become a lifestyle or stronghold in your life.

Therefore, this area of the book will make you identify, examine, expose or beware of the set-up of Satan. People just don't realize that Satan uses the same old tricks against us all the time. We just go through cycles over and over as Satan presents different people in our lives to use and abuse us over and over in various ways. Satan's goal is to keep us trapped and bound. Unless you wake up and learn to see Satan for who he truly is, you'll keep repeating the hopeless issues of life.

So, the decision is up to you to journey to victory. If and when you turn this very page, the door will be open to conquer the issues of your life. Please enter and expose the demons that transfer themselves throughout generations.

In and Out The Dugout

In and Out The Dugout

Life Exposure 1
Young Lady

We as young ladies, often asked ourselves, "Why can't I find me a good man?" There's only one answer to that question. The Bible speaks when a man finds a WIFE he finds a good thing. (Not when a woman finds a HUSBAND she finds a good thing.)

Some hunters (men) see your loneliness and feed off it. For example, when a man speaks to a woman, an aroma comes off of her and a good hunter can sift her out. This means she shows some signs of being vulnerable.

Some ladies get involved in a relationship according to the outer appearance of a man. We all know that what looks good to you is not good for you. After a woman gets involved in the relationship for about a year, the hidden demon that has been silenced comes out. That means the man manifests himself. (It is the true him.)

The same cycle repeats itself more than once. Why? We look for the same appetite in another person. We don't take the time to focus our attention on self.

Some ladies feel like being alone means they're not attractive to the opposite sex. Some ladies feel like their body can attract a good man. (Some outer appearance speaks for what it is.) We as young ladies don't leave anything for the man's imagination. Sometimes what you see is what you get. If a hunter (man) sees a fine body, if he stays around long enough he will catch the prey (woman).

Some young ladies get involved with a drug dealer for money. We all know that a drug dealer loves women, money, and a fast lifestyle. The flip side to a drug dealer is a premature grave or jail. Very few make it out.

The young lady who gets involved with a drug dealer sometimes recycles the seed. (BABIES). Our babies are a product of the parents.

Life Exposure 2
Single Man

Single man: unmarried: without a wife.

A single man should have a desire to have a wife. He should long for a lady to have as a wife one day. The word states that God would make a wife for Adam that would help him to achieve the destination to which God has intended. ***(Genesis 2:18) The Lord said, "It is not good for man to be alone. I will make a companion for him that will help him.."***

A single man should have a hard time getting his needs met if he's not married especially if the woman meeting his needs is not his mother. Why? For example, a young man 25 years old has his own apartment and several female friends. He never goes to the laundry or prepares his own meals. He has a different female over to his apartment every night or twice a day. He never gets the opportunity to long for a wife. The young ladies are always meeting his physical and emotional desires. Why should he make a commitment when he can get the same benefit without it?

Life Exposure 3
Married Man

Married man: united with a wife, joined, put together
Appetite: physical craving; instinctive physical desire; strong wish, urge; hunger or thirst; sexual desires

Some married men have a problem with their wives. His problems are not always with the wife, 5 times out of 10 it's the man fault.

Some men who are married don't have a problem with being married. Their problem is being faithful in the marriage. One of the reasons why a man has the problem is that of his whorish nature. This nature started long before a lady becomes his wife. Some men feel like if they take care of home, they're free to do what they want.

Any single lady who gets involved with a married man is only getting USED. I heard a married man tell a lady, "Why should I bring sand to the beach? When it's plenty out here." This is a powerful statement the man made but the lady didn't comprehend.

It doesn't matter how many bills he pays or how much money he gives you. You are still being USED. Why? He is satisfying his own personal appetite.

Life Exposure 4
I Took Him from His Wife

Getting involved with a married man is wrong. Some ladies get so deeply involved with a married man. They cause problems with his marriage. Some of the problems they may cause are downright disrespectful. In fact, both parties are disrespectful to each other. The man is lying causing disruption in the home. After a period of time the wife separates or divorces the husband. The ladies' goal is accomplished.

Here is an example for a clearer understanding: A couple has been married for about 15 years. Within the 15 years of marriage, he has always secretly cheated on his wife. This involvement is different because it became an open affair. (**He's disrespectful with it.**)

After going through years of hell, the wife decides to leave. She wants to spend the rest of her life in peace. Then the other woman thinks her goal is accomplished. The real deal is the wife was tired. After 15 years of marriage and the wife decide to divorce, that speaks for itself.

The Bible speaks of reaping what you sow. (**What I'm saying is, what you give out is what you will get back.**)

Life Exposure 5
Player

Player: an actor; a performer; a person who is skilled.
Stigma: a disgrace; a mark; a spot; a scar.

Some men like the reputation of having more than one woman. Why? He's battling with hidden low self esteem and rejection. A real player is so upfront that he will tell the women he has another girlfriend besides her.

Some ladies are so physically moved; she thinks that if she gets involved with him she could change his ways. A lady cannot change a player; she is just another notch in his belt.

Some men have a way of making women pay for their needs being met. Players call that "**HAVING GAMES**"

Men who call themselves players cover their tracks very well. They can have two ladies living close to one another and the ladies will never know about each other.

A man who is a player is the most dangerous person to get involved with. Why? He leaves a stigma on the lady marking her as a fool. These women are usually known around town as a "**MARK.**"

Another reason to beware of a player or to stop being a player is the risk of contracting diseases that go along with

In and Out The Dugout

having multiple partners. You don't have to be a player to contract a disease, but if your are, the odds are against you.

There's one thing a player does not know, the strongest game is played by the weakest player.

Life Exposure 6
Old Man Who Looks for A Young Prey

An older man has mastered the game and has turned out to be an excellent hunter. One of his most exciting thrills is getting involved with a young lady. Some older men will only date younger ladies. The reason for this is to impress his friends. The friend will praise him by using the words: "**HE STUCK AGAIN.**"

When a younger lady dates an older man, it's for financial reasons. (**She calls him her SUGAR DADDY.**) After dating an older man, the young lady's youth is slowly drained. Her appearance is slowly changing. (This also goes for a young man who dates an older woman.)

Some older men hang out in the nightclubs waiting to catch his next prey. Here's one way you can identify a hunter. He's very distinguished, well-groomed, dresses well and is an excellent dancer. He's the man that would buy you a drink that will cost you more in the long run. He's the demon that will sit in the club and prey on all generations.

Life Exposure 7
My First Boyfriend

Seed: multi-cellular structure where things are reproduced; the condition of having or proceeding to form, the beginning or germ to produce.
Strongholds: a fastness of fortified refuge; a place where anything is in great strength.
Transfer: to carry or bring over
Vulnerable: capable of being physically or emotional wounded. Capable of being persuaded or tempted.

Some teenage girls get involved at an early age and lose their virginity. After becoming sexually involved with a young man, a young girl's life is turned upside down. (**She's in love.**) Different levels of hell start to take place in her life.

This act has become a game to the young man. He continues this cycle until he finds someone to become his wife in the later years.

The one who loses her virginity goes through emotional changes or gets pregnant. These changes can repeat with different males, the one she loses her virginity to causes mental pain in her life. She allows him to continue running in and out of her life because of the sexual connection or stronghold. **(Stronghold: a place where anything is in great strength.)**

When a teenager enters the sex arena, she opens the door that recycles itself in different ways.

Life Exposure 8
He Got A Child While We Were Dating

During the course of dating, some men will cheat in their relationship and father a child with another woman. We as women often blame the other lady, not the man. *(Saying she got that baby on purpose.)* We all know that it takes two to tango. Some ladies have a hard time adjusting to the fact, it happened and she can't change it.

So she stays in the relationship, sometimes it's according to the outer appearance. The lady may ask a question, but never comprehend the question she asked. Some questions you ask paints a bigger picture of the person you want to get involved with.

For example, if you asked a man how many kids he has before dating him. His answer is four and three baby's mamas never been married. That should tell you the nature of the person you would be getting yourself involved with. This nature started long before she got involved with him.

She fell in the trap and became emotionally involved. This trap can recycle itself in different relationships. **(Same script but a different cast..)**

Life Exposure 9
We Live Together

We as women feel like if he moves in with us, then the relationship is secure. *(WRONG)* The relationship is not secure. If you stay in a relationship long enough, all hell will break loose. The Bible speaks of a marriage, not a live-in relationship.

For example, say a couple has been dating for about seven months and things are really going well. He begins to leave shoes and clothes at her house. Her emotions are running wild. *(Now she's in love)* She secures her position in his life by allowing him to move in her home.

The first three months, he comes in every night at a decent time. Shortly after that he comes in the house late. One of the excuses is he hanging out with the boys. The next weekend the time gets later.

This problem is now repeating itself every other weekend. The hidden demon has manifest. (**CAME OUT**) Her life has been turned around. She stays in the relationship hoping things will get better. In situations like this, things never get better.

In this example, he never makes the type of commitment she wants. Why buy the cow when you can get the milk for free? Why make a commitment when you can already reap the benefits of a marriage? We as women let our emotions make the decisions and don't make the right choice.

Life Exposure 10
He Raped Me

Rape: unlawful sexual intercourse (by force or technically, with a minor) with another person without that person's consent; violation, despoliation or to violate.

Rape is a very serious crime. Rape causes pain in an area that only God can restore. One of the most common forms of rape today is date rape. There are several types of rapes. All rape violates the person's life. It's wrong for someone to take something without your permission. Date rape has become the most prevalent rape today among young people. One reason is because of their immoral actions.

For example, when a young lady and a young man meet and start dating, the couple may talk on the phone for weeks or months. After several conversations on the phone the conversation shifts to a different level. This level is sexual. This is the most dangerous level to enter. The conversations begin to heat up and hormones kick in. This tension may build up for two weeks or more.

The young lady knows the young man's outer appearance; yet she never discerns the person she's really talking to on the phone. The couple meets at a party; she's trying to impress her friends by making the statement that's my man. She allows him to kiss her and show her sexual gestures.

After the party, the couple goes into a private area. She's playing a role as if she is going to have sex with him. The young man's emotions are out of control. In the heat of the moment, she wants to get out of the problem she's created, but he forces his way and takes the game to the next level. *(It's taken without permission)* She cries out rape, and ended up like some ladies who create their problems by playing with the opposite sex's emotions. In this way, these ladies provoke their own destruction. **YES,** it was wrong for him to force himself without her permission, AND it was **WRONG** for her to play games with his emotions.

When you open up doors and enter into the **DEVIL'S** campgrounds, do not expect to be treated fairly. The devil's whole objective is to rob, kill, steal and destroy.

There are some rapes that you have no control over. It is wrong, but the one you create is the one that you can prevent. How? **DON'T CREATE IT.**

Life Exposure 11
My Man Is In Prison
(He has 20 years to Life)

We've all heard the saying the mind is a terrible thing to waste. There are so many ways that the mind can be wasted and controlled. A man that meets a woman while in prison has mentally established a method that controls his prey *(the woman)*, without a physical touch. He learned how to master the appetite of the individual. He knows how to make her feel important without laying his hands on her. This person carries a Jezebel spirit: this spirit controls the individual's life in many different ways.

There are some men that go to prison and control the female's life. When he gets out, he finds a new relationship to get involved in. Women who get involved or stay with a man while he is in prison generally have low self-esteem. She does not value her self-worth; she creates her own prison ministry.

She visits the prison four times a month and sends money to him. He calls her on a regular basis. This demon has learned to master the mind and control his prey.

Life Exposure 12
He Beat Me But He Love Me

Some relationships that you get involved in have hidden angers with it. Once the anger is exposed, it continues on in the relationship. When this demon exposes itself, it is hard getting the individual out of your life.

This anger can elevate to a different level which can cost you your life. If a man hits you in the right place one time, he can take your life.

Sometimes a man feels like if he can't control you, he will beat you. The lady will use the phrase *(he beat me because he loves me.)* Some men will fight a woman. When it comes to a man, he will back down.

Some men think he has to have a certain level of respect in order to be a man. If he can't control the female, he will beat her until she respects his authority as a man. Respect is earned from a person, not beaten out of them. We all know a man can overpower the woman physically, but mentally he is no match for the lady. Both mental and physical abuse is dangerous for the mind and body.

Life Exposure 13
Your Girlfriend Who You Talk To

During a crisis we turn to our girlfriends for help. Little do we know the life of the girlfriend who we are talking to is in worse shape. During the conversation you find out she has more problem in her life than you. Before the conversation ends, you both are having a pity party. Some of the advice that the girlfriend gives during a crisis can add more fuel to the fire, especially when she has not experienced the hurt you're in.

As you read in the book, there's a friend you can turn to that can deliver you and change your life. That friend is Jesus.

Life Exposure 14
Your Friend's Boyfriend

A true friendship can last a lifetime. When the opposite sex is involved, it can cause division in the friendship. It causes one to have to choose between the friendship and the relationship. The relationship is chosen because of sexual involvement.

The friendship is destroyed. The character and reputation of both individuals is ruined. The friends have become victims. The one who stays involved in the relationship goes through hell. She continues to go through hell until one day she says enough is enough.

Sometimes the person never gets enough, she marries the boyfriend and hell continues in the marriage. The man destroys the reputation and the friendship.

For example, when two people are friends, and one is in a relationship. The boyfriend takes advantage of the friend. The boyfriend exposes the friend, but the friend who is innocent gets accused. *(John 8: 1-11) Jesus returned to the Mount of Olives, but early the next morning he was back again at the Temple. A crowd soon gathered, and he sat down and taught them. As he was speaking, the teachers of religious law and Pharisees brought a woman they had* caught in the act of adultery. They put her in front of the crowd.

"Teacher," they said to Jesus, "this woman was caught in the very act of adultery. The law of Moses says to stone her. What do you say?" They were trying to trap him into saying something they could use against him, but Jesus stooped down and wrote in the dust with his finger. They kept demanding an answer, so he stood up again and said, "All right, stone her. But let those who have never sinned throw the first stones!" Then he stooped down again and wrote in the dust. When the accusers heard this, they slipped away one by one, beginning with the oldest, until only Jesus was left in the middle of the crowd with the woman. Then Jesus stood up again and said to her, "Where are your accusers? Didn't even on of them condemn you?" "No, Lord," she said. And Jesus said, "Neither do I. Go and sin no more."

It's hard to fight when you have been violated. When the flesh is getting satisfaction, I call that **caviar,** a very expensive appetizer that can cost you. When the opposite sex is involved, the friendship will turn into a nightmare.

Life Exposure 15
The Young Man's Mother

Sometimes a woman feels like she should become friends with a man's mother. The mother can control her son's behavior. Someone before her tried the same trick. This behavior or nature was given to him from a seed form. Before he entered this world, he is a product of his parents' lifestyle.

Some mothers are straight and will tell a young lady not to get involved with her son. There are some that will watch you get hurt because of the pain she went through. Some mothers will play along with the game for her own personal craving.

Life Exposure 16
That's My Baby's Daddy

"That's my baby's daddy" has became a very popular statement. Some women who have a baby's daddy allow him to continue coming in and out of her life. It's not for the child's welfare, but for her emotional needs. Some men feel like they have the right to come in and out of the lady's life. (**One day a man told me it was good to have a baby's mama or two because they can always go back to play house with her.**) This statement had become real throughout women's lives. Ladies who have a baby's daddy or two have a beginning and end to all of her chapters.

In and Out The Dugout

READY TO GIVE UP YOUR PAST?

I know that it was difficult to have your life exposed right in front of your eyes. Sometimes the truth about ourselves and our struggles can hurt us so deeply because we don't realize that we are in such bad shape. The good news is that Jesus is a healer. If you surrender and give your life to Him, He will make you whole again. He will heal you, deliver you, and restore your dignity and self-respect. Won't you continue on your journey to victory in Jesus Christ? If so, turn the page and Jesus and I will be there to meet you *on the winning side!*

In and Out The Dugout

In and Out The Dugout

Respect

Respect: to treat with consideration; to feel or show esteem; to value

Respect starts with self. Once you value yourself, you will demand no less than respect. You will come to a point where you will give respect and demand to receive respect.

Sometime it takes experiences after experiences for someone to come to a point a change needs to be made. Respect demands boundaries to be set in your life. (***Boundaries: a limit; a border; termination; final limit.***) Respect is a key tool. It carries a strong demand of life. Life changes can repeat or recycle if the person has low self-esteem.

Some actions and experiences can cause a person to go into denial. Some denials can lead up to revenge. We cause our own self-destruction because we want to get the person who did us wrong. The reason why is because of lack of respect for ourselves. We blame other people for the problems we cause. We often look at the outer appearance, and never discern or comprehend the motive of the person.

Once you face the fact that you brought some situations upon yourself, the healing process will start to take place in your life. That's when you know you are almost out of the dugout....

Repentance

True: faithful, genuine, agreeing with facts.
Repentance: to change from past evil or misconduct.

Once you develop respect and set boundaries you will come to a level of change. This level requires repenting not I'm sorry. We often tell God we're sorry and do the same thing over again. The reason we pray and tell God we're sorry is because of the situation we created.

For example, two friends go to a club and one gets very intoxicated. She returns home from the club. She's up all night praying and telling God, she will never do this again. The next day she gets a call that Frank is having a house party and she attends. The cycle repeats itself because of the temporary satisfaction. *(Galatians 5: 19-21) When you follow the desires of your sinful nature, your lives will produce these evil results: sexual immorality, impure thoughts, eagerness for lustful pleasure, idolatry, participation in demonic activities, hostility, quarreling, jealousy, outbursts of anger, selfish ambition, divisions, the feeling that everyone is wrong except those in your own little group, envy drunkenness, wild parties, and other kinds of sin. Let me tell you again, as I have before, that anyone living that sort of life will not inherit the Kingdom of God.*

When you get to that point where you want a change not a temporary satisfaction. You will give God a true repentance, not a worldly I'm sorry. The words I'm sorry are a turn around statement. Why?

I'm: contraction of I am
Sorry: express pity, sympathy (worthless)

Therefore, the statement I'm sorry (beg pardon) is temporary, but a true repentance means: **" Give Up!"**

True: faithful, genuine, agreeing with facts
Repentance: to change from past evil or misconduct.

God can use difficulties to encourage us to repent. *(2 Corinthians 7: 9-10) Now I am glad I sent it not because it hurt you, but because the pain caused you to have remorse and change your ways. It was the kind of sorrow God wants his people to have, so you were not harmed by us in anyway, For God can use sorrow in our lives to help us turn away from sin and seek salvation. We will regret that kind of sorrow. But sorrow without repentance is the kind that results to death,*

God will punish those who do not turn from their sin. Turning from sin means confession and repenting. Confession of sin accompanies a changed lifestyle.

In the next chapter you are ready to go see a man who is ready to reform you.

Reform: to form again or in a new way. To transform, to make better, to remove defects from: to bring to a better way of life, to abandon evil ways.

(2 Chronicles 7:14) Then if my people who are called by my name will humble themselves and pray and seek my face and turn from their wicked ways, I will forgive their sin and heal their land.

JESUS

The Master Key of Deliverance

When you come to a point in your life that friends and relatives you talk to run out of solutions or the man you turned who fill avoid for a limited time, you are tired of that temporary satisfaction. There's a man who can make a deposit in your life and no devil in hell can make a withdrawal. His name is **JESUS**. **"Come, see a man, which told me all things that even I did: is not this the Christ?"**

Jesus has the authority over all demons. *(Mark 1: 23-26) 23 A man possessed by an evil spirit was in the synagogue, 24 and he began shouting, "Why are you bothering us, Jesus of Nazareth? Have you come to destroy us? I know who you are –the Holy One sent from God!" 25 Jesus cut him short, "be silent! Come out of the man." 26 A that, the evil spirit screamed and threw the man into a convulsion, but then he left him.*

Jesus suffered and went to the cross for everything we need. Jesus' blood paid the price to free people who believe. Jesus is the only one who can break the repeated cycles in your life. Jesus is perfect in his love, peace, patience, joy and all the other fruits of the spirit embodied in one single person.

Jesus is the author of life. He gives life. Jesus will restore and replace the void in your life. Jesus gives peace that surpasses all human understanding. God is not only the Father, but He is everything you need Him to be. When you truly give your life to Jesus, He can use you in a way that you cannot imagine.

We've played ball on the wrong team for too many years. Satan will use and keep you in the dugout (**pit**). Temptation is Satan's primary weapon to destroy us. Satan is very predictable. The first thing that Satan does is identify the desires in you. He then feeds off desires and keeps you repeating cycles. He uses the same strategy and old tricks just new people.

Sitting in the dugout never gives you the opportunity to play ball. Once upon a time, I was kept confined for Satan's use. Back then, I used to think I was free because I was living on my own, but really, I was bound. When I gave my life to Jesus, it freed me from captivity. Now my old lifestyle and desires have changed. The same thing can happen to you when you give your life to Jesus because Jesus gives you liberty and power to walk all over the devil. **Liberty: freedom from captivity; slavery; unrestrained enjoyment of natural of rights.**

That's when you know you are out of the dugout (**PIT**). You're on the winning team when you give your life to Christ. Jesus can take nothing and make something out of it. When the devil thinks he got you, Jesus steps up and calls your name. *(John 11:39-44) 39 "Roll the stone aside." Jesus told them. But Martha, the dead man's sister, said, "Lord, by now the smell will be terrible because he has been dead for four days." 40 Jesus respond, "Didn't I tell you that you will see God's glory if you believe?" 41 So they rolled the stone aside. Then Jesus looked up to heaven and said, "Father, thank you for hearing me. 42 You always hear me, but I said it out loud for the sake of all these people standing here, so they will believe you sent me." 43 Then Jesus shouted, "Lazarus, come out!" 44 And Lazarus came out, bound in grave clothes, his face wrapped in a head cloth. Jesus told them, "Unwrap him and let him go!"*

You will not just be a member on the team; you will have a position that is dangerous to the kingdom of darkness. This position gives you the opportunity not just to hit a home run, but the authority to hit a grand slam **(to bring other home to Jesus).** Your life will change and you will become a person with morals and standards.

The things that happened to you were written in God's book before you were born. *(Jeremiah 1: 5) "I knew you before I formed you in your mother's womb. Before you were born I set you apart and appointed you as my spokesman to the world.* All the pain in your life will make you find your way to Jesus. Jesus is the only one who can take the shackles off your arms and legs set you free.

God is the only one who can take something bad and make it a testimony to help someone else learn to glorify Him.

EPILOGUE

In and Out The Dugout

Jesus and the Samaritan Woman
(John 4: 6-29)

Jacob's well was there; and Jesus, tired from the long walk, sat wearily beside the well about noontime. Soon a Samaritan woman came to draw water, and Jesus said to her, " *Please give me a drink."* He was alone at the time because his disciples had gone into the village to buy some food.

The woman was surprised, for Jews refused to have anything to do with Samaritans. She said to Jesus, "You are a Jew, and I am a Samaritan woman. Why are you asking me for a drink?" Jesus replied, *"If you only knew the gift of God had for you and who I am. You would ask me, and I would give you living water."*

"But sir, you don't have a rope or a bucket," she said, "and this is a very deep well. Where would you get this living water? And besides, are you greater than our ancestor Jacob who gave us this well? How can you offer better water than he and his sons and his cattle enjoyed?"

Jesus replied, *"People soon become thirsty again after drinking this water. But the water I give them takes away spring within them, giving them eternal life."* "Please, sir," the woman said, "give me some of that water! Then I'll never be thirsty again, and I won't have to come here to haul water."

"Go get you husband," Jesus told her. "I don't have a husband," the woman replied. Jesus said, "You're right! You don't have a husband- for you have five husbands and you aren't even married to the man you're living with now."

"Sir," the woman said. "you must be a prophet. So tell me, why is it that you Jews insist that Jerusalem is the only place of worship, while we Samaritans claim it is here at Mount Gerizim, * where our ancestors worshiped?"

Jesus replied, "Believe me, the time is coming when it will no longer matter whether you worship the Father here or in Jerusalem. You Samaritans know so little about the one you worship, while we Jews know all about him, for salvation comes and is already here when true worshipers will worship the Father in spirit and in truth. The Father is looking for anyone who will worship him that way. For God is Spirit, so those who worship him must worship in spirit and in truth."

The woman said, " I know the Messiah will come-the one who is called Christ. When he comes, he will explain everything to us." Then Jesus told her, " **I am the Messiah!** "*

Just then his disciples arrived. They were astonished to find him talking to a woman, but none of them asked him why he was doing it or what they had been discussing. The woman left her water jar beside the well and went back to the village and told everyone, **"COME AND SEE A MAN WHO TOLD ME EVERYTHING I EVER DID! CAN THIS BE THE MESSIAH?"**

GLOSSARY
"Webster's Dictionary"

Curse: to invoke or wish evil upon another

Cycle: a period of time in which an event happens in a certain order, which constantly repeats itself.

Deliverance: set free, to rescue from evil or free discharge; to hand over.

Dugout: a place where one waits when not in a game. Pit of hell

Generation: originating people of the same descendants. Removed from the same number of steps from a common ancestor.

Hunter: a person or animal that hunts; seek out, chases

Identify: to see clearly, pinpoint

In: those who repeat or enter (repeated cycle)

Liberty: freedom from captivity, slavery

Manifest: easily seen by the eye or perceived by the mind, the act of showing something publicly, to reveal

Out: a way from inside, not in use, not to be considered; no longer a part of

Prey: killed and eaten by another, a victim, to live on as a victim

Recycle: to pass again through a series of changes.

Reform: to form again or in a new way; to transform, to make better, to remove defects from; to bring to a better way of life, to abandon evil ways

Dear Reader,

I am honored to have had the opportunity to share my life with you. This book, In and Out the Dugout: The Encyclopedia of Street Life, talks about the life I once lived. We all have a story to tell, a book deep within us that needs to be birthed out to help someone else. It is my prayer that God ministered to your hearts through the words of my testimony.

My friend, I encourage you to stay prayerful knowing that your deliverance is on the way. Remember God is a forgiving God who will forgive our sins, if we confess them. If we say we have no sin, we are only fooling ourselves and refusing to accept the truth. But if we confess our sins to Him, He is faithful and just to forgive us and to cleanse us from every wrong. (I John 1:8-9)

Moreover, God is no respecter of persons, and is faithful to the just and the unjust. However, when you make the choice to submit to His will for your life and live for Him, God can take what Satan meant for evil in your life and use it for His glory. Therefore, I pray that you will accept Jesus Christ as your Lord and Savior. Let Him complete the great work in you.

May God bless and keep you in perfect peace.

Yours in Christ,

Cathy Howard

ACKNOWLEDGEMENTS

Pastor Henry and Patricia Phillips you allowed God to use your lives and His word to empower people to turn from their wicked ways and to live by the principles of God's Holy Word. God has placed you in this region to impact the truth and His words in peoples' lives so they can be set free from captivity. They can find their destiny and purposes for their lives. The Bible speaks that His sheep will know Him by His voice. You are truly shepherds from God.

My son Tyrunne who has been a joy in my life, your sweet soft words have encouraged me in difficult times when you didn't understand the things mother was going through.

Just like God used Mary to birth Jesus, Minnie Howard was the vessel that God used to bring me in the world. Before I was born, God knew that Minnie was going to birth Cathy, and I thank God for my mother.

Diane, Delorse, Edgar, Tommie Jr., Gidget, Nicole, and the late Fernaldo Howard, life wasn't a bed of roses growing up but it is worth living.

The late Tommie Lee Howard Sr. who supported his family in all crises whether they were good or bad: his love opened up doors and caused his family to press beyond his death. He was an ultimate dad.

Sarah Degraffenried naturally is my cousin. God has birthed a relationship far beyond a cousin. It's a spiritual connection made from heaven.

Beverly Wilson, your support as a friend has reached a level that no one was able to reach in years. God has placed you in my life to witness the metamorphosis that has taken place in me.

SPECIAL THANKS

Gwen Campbell/Artist
Thank you for allowing God to use you to bring my vision to pass.

Kevin King/ Co-Worker
Kevin, you allowed God to use your ears to hear scriptures that were needed to bring the book to pass.

Bridgette Pratts/Editor
You came in my life to edit this book. God used you as a midwife to help position and turn what was in me so that I wouldn't have a premature birth while giving birth to this book.

Edna Farmer/Editor
Your years of experience were needed for a first time writer. Thank you for taking the time out of your busy schedule to review my book.

Masa Waddell/ Chief Editor
Now that I'm in the right position to give birth to this book, it was you who has taken the responsibility to clean it up for the world to see.

Pastor Charlie and Rose Alexander
My way wasn't God's way. The way he put you in my life was divine. Pastor Rose is also the author of "Jesus Is A Match Maker" and "Maternity Leave."

Remarks

Cathy stay encouraged, God is truly on your side. I've seen a metamorphosis take place in your life. To see God's wonderful work come out of you blesses me.
Ann MacFarland

Cathy, I've worked with you for many years. I know the old you, and I was able to witness God's wonder and the change He made in you. It was like a butterfly coming out of a cocoon. Many didn't understand but God knew what He was doing.
Beverly Wilson

Cathy, many saw it but didn't want to believe it. It speaks for itself. I saw the old you turn into a whole new person. Stay encouraged and continue on with your journey in Christ.
Marcelle Goliday-Blackmon

In and Out The Dugout

Your Reflections

In and Out The Dugout

Your Reflections

In and Out The Dugout

Your Reflections

In and Out The Dugout

Your Reflections

In and Out The Dugout

YOU CAN PICK-UP BOOKS AT:

POWER OF CHANGE CHRISTIAN CENTER BOOKSTORE
610 Range Lane
Cahokia, Illinois 62206

Order Online: www.pocccbookstore.org

CANDY BOUTIQUE
5200 North Illinois
Suite 104
Fairview Heights, Illinois 62208

Check your Local Bookstore

In and Out The Dugout

To obtain books, complete and mail the information below.

(Please print)

Name_____

Address_____

City_____

State_____ Zip_____

Mail to:
    Cathy Howard
    P. O. Box 23216
    Belleville, Illinois 62226

Make checks or money orders payable to Cathy Howard. Price $ 9.95 + applicable sales tax.

If you order by mail add $2.00 for shipping & handling.